BASICS OF KEYBOARD THEORY

LEVEL III

Fourth Edition

Julie McIntosh Johnson

J. Johnson Music Publications

5062 Siesta Ln.
Yorba Linda, CA 92886
(714) 961-0257

Basics of Keyboard Theory, Level III, Fourth Edition

Published by:

J. Johnson Music Publications
5062 Siesta Ln.
Yorba Linda, CA 92886 U.S.A.
(714) 961-0257

©1997 by Julie McIntosh Johnson. Revised.
Previous editions ©1983, 1990, and 1992, Julie McIntosh Johnson.
Printed by KNI Inc., Anaheim, California, United States of America

Library of Congress Cataloging in Publication Data

Johnson, Julie Anne McIntosh
Basics of Keyboard Theory, Level III, Fourth Edition

ISBN 1-891757-03-2 $8.95 Softcover, comb binding

LC TX 4-721-494

TO THE TEACHER

Intended as a supplement to private or group music lessons, *Basics of Keyboard Theory, Level III* presents basic theory concepts to the early intermediate music student. This level is to be used with the student has had approximately 3-4 years of music lessons, and is playing piano literature at the level of Clementi's *Sonatina, Op. 36, No. 1*, or Burgmuller's *Arabesque*.

Basics of Keyboard Theory, Level III is divided into 11 lessons, with several reviews, and a test at the end. Lessons may be combined with one another or divided into smaller sections, depending on the ability of the student. Whenever possible, it is helpful to demonstrate theory concepts on the keyboard, and apply them to the music the student is playing.

Learning music theory can be a very rewarding experience for the student when carefully applied to the lessons. *Basics of Keyboard Theory, Level III*, is an important part of learning this valuable subject.

BASICS OF KEYBOARD THEORY
COMPUTER ACTIVITIES
by
Nancy Plourde
with
Julie McIntosh Johnson and Anita Yee Belansky

Colorful, exciting games that reinforce Basics of Keyboard Theory lessons!

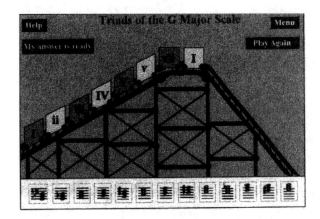

LEVELS PREPARATORY, 1, and 2: 30 GAMES, 10 PER LEVEL!
LEVELS 3 and 4: 20 GAMES, 10 PER LEVEL!
LEVELS 5 and 6: 20 GAMES, 10 PER LEVEL!
Corresponds with MTAC CM Syllabus & *Basics of Keyboard Theory* books, or may be used independently.

Download a free demo at www.pbjmusic.com

--**Order Form**--

Name_____

Address_____

City_____State_____Zip_____

Email_____Phone_____

Mail to: PBJ Music Publications
5062 Siesta Ln.
Yorba Linda, CA 92886
(714) 961-0257

Qty		Cost
_____	Levels Prep-II, Mac/PC: $49.95	_____
_____	Levels III-IV, Mac/PC: $39.95	_____
_____	Levels 5-6, PC only: $49.95	_____
	Sub Total:	_____
	Sales Tax (CA, AZ, TX residents)	_____
	Shipping:	$4.00
	Total:	_____

System Requirements

IBM or compatible: 486 33 MHz or higher, Windows 3.1, 95, 98, NT, or XP, 8 MB RAM, 5 MB hard disk space, MIDI Soundcard, VGA monitor.

Macintosh: System 7 or greater, 8 MB RAM, 3 MB hard disk space available, color monitor.

TABLE OF CONTENTS

Basics of Keyboard Theory is dedicated to my husband Rob, without whose love, support, help, and incredible patience, this series would not have been possible.

LESSON 1
MAJOR KEY SIGNATURES

At the beginning of a musical composition, there is a **KEY SIGNATURE**. It is next to the clef signs.

The **KEY SIGNATURE** tells you two things:

    1. The key or tonality of the music.

    2. Which notes in the music are to receive sharps or flats.

SHARPS   **FLATS**   **NO SHARPS OR FLATS**

                                         (Key of C Major)

If a key signature has **SHARPS**, they will be written in this order, on these lines and spaces. This is called the **ORDER OF SHARPS.**

FCGDAEB

A saying to help you remember this order is:

Fat Cats Go Down Alleys Eating Bologna

If a key signature has one sharp, it will be F♯. If a key signature has two sharps, they will be F♯ and C♯, etc.

1. Fill in the blanks.

a. If a key signature has two sharps, they will be __F♯__ and __C♯__.

b. If a key signature has three sharps, they will be __F♯__, __C♯__, and __G♯__.

c. If a key signature has one sharp, it will be __F♯__.

d. If a key signature has four sharps, they will be __F♯__, __C♯__, __G♯__, and __B♯__.

2. Write the **ORDER OF SHARPS** three times on the staff below, in both clefs.

To find out which Major key a group of sharps represents, find and name the last sharp (the sharp furthest to the right), then go up a half step from that sharp. The note which is a half step above the last sharp is the name of the Major key.

Three sharps: F♯, C♯, G♯

Last sharp is G♯

A half step above G♯ is A

Key of A Major

3. Name these Major keys.

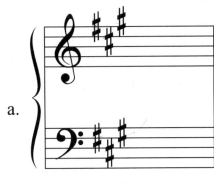

1. The sharps are *F*, *C*, and *G♯*.

2. The last sharp is ____.

3. A half step above this sharp is ____.

4. Key of ____ Major.

a.

1. The sharps is ____.

2. The last sharp is ____.

3. A half step above this sharp is ____.

4. Key of ____ Major.

b.

1. The sharps are ____ and ____.

2. The last sharp is ____.

3. A half step above this sharp is ____.

4. Key of ____ Major.

c.

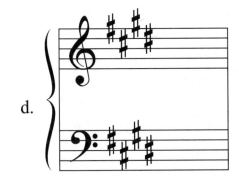

1. The sharps are ____, ____, ____, and ____.

2. The last sharp is ____.

3. A half step above this sharp is ____.

4. Key of ____ Major.

d.

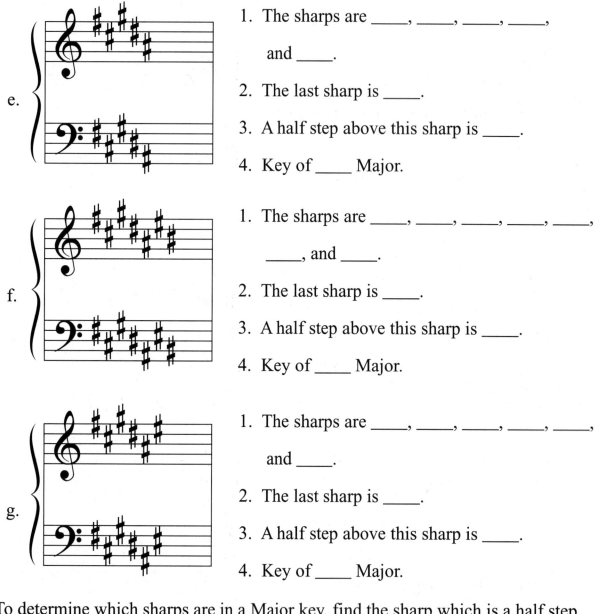

e.

1. The sharps are ____, ____, ____, ____, and ____.

2. The last sharp is ____.

3. A half step above this sharp is ____.

4. Key of ____ Major.

f.

1. The sharps are ____, ____, ____, ____, ____, ____, and ____.

2. The last sharp is ____.

3. A half step above this sharp is ____.

4. Key of ____ Major.

g.

1. The sharps are ____, ____, ____, ____, ____, and ____.

2. The last sharp is ____.

3. A half step above this sharp is ____.

4. Key of ____ Major.

To determine which sharps are in a Major key, find the sharp which is a half step below the name of the key. Name all the sharps from the order of sharps up to and including that sharp.

Key of D Major

A half step below D is C♯

Name all sharps, from the order of sharps, up to and including C♯

F♯ and C♯

4. Write the key signatures for these keys.

   a. Key of A Major

      1. A half step below A is _____.

      2. The order of sharps up to this sharp

         is _____, _____, _____.

      3. Write these sharps on the staff in both clefs.

   b. Key of G Major

      1. A half step below G is _____.

      2. The order of sharps up to this sharp

         is _____.

      3. Write this sharp on the staff in both clefs.

   c. Key of E Major

      1. A half step below E is _____.

      2. The order of sharps up to this sharp

         is _____, _____, _____, _____.

      3. Write these sharps on the staff in both clefs.

   d. Key of F♯ Major

      1. A half step below F♯ is _____.

      2. The order of sharps up to this sharp

         is _____, _____, _____, _____, _____, _____.

      3. Write these sharps on the staff in both clefs.

e. Key of D Major

   1. A half step below D is _____.

   2. The order of sharps up to this sharp

      is _____, _____.

   3. Write these sharps on the staff in both clefs.

f. Key of C♯ Major

   1. A half step below C♯ is _____.

   2. The order of sharps up to this sharp

      is _____, _____, _____, _____, _____,

      _____, _____.

   3. Write these sharps on the staff in both clefs.

g. Key of B Major

   1. A half step below B is _____.

   2. The order of sharps up to this sharp

      is _____, _____, _____, _____, _____.

   3. Write these sharps on the staff in both clefs.

5. Match these key signatures with their names by drawing lines to connect them.

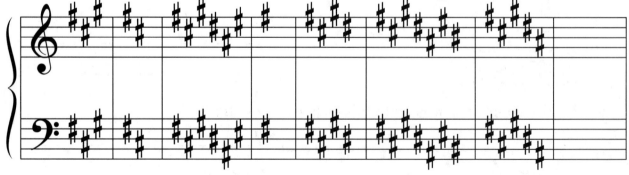

D Major F♯ Major A Major C Major C♯ Major G Major E Major B Major

6. Memorize these key signatures.

    C Major has no sharps or flats.
    G Major has F♯.
    D Major has F♯ and C♯.
    A Major has F♯, C♯, and G♯.
    E Major has F♯, C♯, G♯, and D♯.
    B Major has F♯, C♯, G♯, D♯, and A♯.
    F♯ Major has F♯, C♯, G♯, D♯, A♯, and E♯
    C♯ Major has F♯, C♯, G♯, D♯, A♯, E♯, and B♯

If a key signature has flats, they will be in the order B♭, E♭, A♭, D♭, G♭, C♭, F♭. This is called the **ORDER OF FLATS.**

THE ORDER OF FLATS

The Order of Flats can be memorized this way: **BEAD Gum Candy Fruit**

If a key signature has one flat, it will be B♭. If it has two flats, they will B♭ and E♭, etc.

7. Fill in the blanks.

    a. If a key signature has two flats, they are _____ and _____.

    b. If a key signature has one flat, it is _____.

    c. If a key signature has three flats, they are _____, _____, and _____.

8. Write the Order of Flats three times on the staff below, in both clefs.

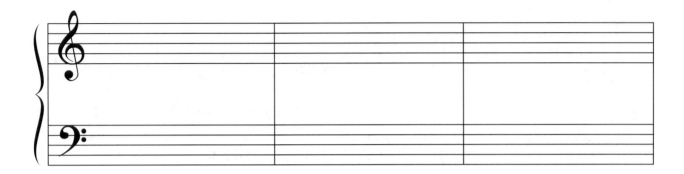

To determine which Major key a group of flats represents, name the next to last flat in the key signature.

Three flats: B♭, E♭, A♭

Next to last flat is E♭

Key of E♭ Major

The key signature for F Major needs to be memorized. It has one flat: B♭.

**KEY SIGNATURE FOR
F MAJOR**

9. Name these Major keys.

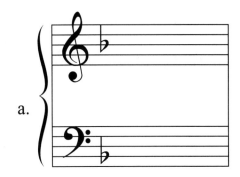

a.

1. One flat: _____.

2. This key signature must be memorized.

3. Key of _____ Major.

b.

1. Two flats: _____ and _____.

2. The next to last flat is _____.

3. Key of _____ Major.

c.

1. Three flats: _____, _____, and _____.

2. The next to last flat is _____.

3. Key of _____ Major.

d.

1. Five flats: _____, _____, _____, _____,

   and _____.

2. The next to last flat is _____.

3. Key of _____ Major.

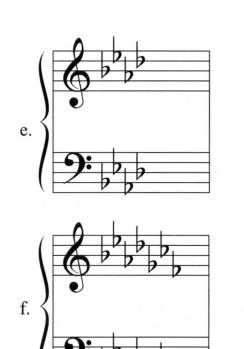

e.

1. Four flats: _____, _____, _____, and _____.

2. The next to last flat is _____.

3. Key of _____ Major.

f.

1. Seven flats: _____, _____, _____, _____,

   _____, _____, and _____.

2. The next to last flat is _____.

3. Key of _____ Major.

g.

1. Six flats: _____, _____, _____, _____,

   _____, and _____.

2. The next to last flat is _____.

3. Key of _____ Major.

To determine which flats are needed for a given Major key, name all the flats from the Order of Flats up to and including the name of the key, then add one more flat.

Key of E♭ Major

Name all flats from the Order of Flats
up to and including E♭, then add one more.

B♭, E♭, and A♭

10. Write the key signatures for these keys. Fill in the blanks, then write the flats for the key signature on the staff <u>in both clefs.</u>

a. Key of B♭ Major

1. Name all flats from the Order of Flats up to and including B♭, then add one more.

2. ____ and ____.

b. Key of E♭ Major

1. Name all flats from the Order of Flats up to and including E♭, then add one more.

2. ____, ____, and ____.

c. Key of F Major

1. Memorize this key signature.

2. ____.

d. Key of G♭ Major

1. Name all flats from the Order of Flats up to and including G♭, then add one more.

2. ____, ____, ____, ____, ____, and ____.

e. Key of A♭ Major

1. Name all flats from the Order of Flats up to and including A♭, then add one more.

2. ____, ____, ____, and ____.

f. Key of C♭ Major

   1. Name all flats from the Order of Flats up to and including C♭, then add one more.

   2. ____, ____, ____, ____, ____,

   ____, and ____.

g. Key of D♭ Major

   1. Name all flats from the Order of Flats up to and including D♭, then add one more.

   2. ____, ____, ____, ____, and ____.

11. Match these key signatures with their names by drawing lines to connect them.

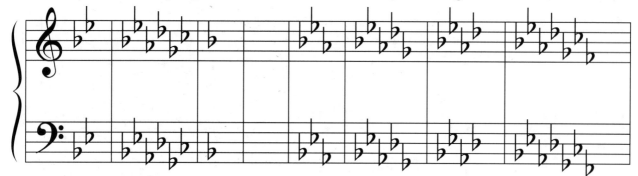

C♭ Major F Major G♭ Major B♭ Major D♭ Major C Major E♭ Major A♭ Major

12. Memorize these key signatures.

F Major has B♭
B♭ Major has B♭, and E♭
E♭ Major has B♭, E♭, and A♭
A♭ Major has B♭, E♭, A♭, and D♭
D♭ Major has B♭, E♭, A♭, D♭, and G♭
G♭ Major has B♭, E♭, A♭, D♭, G♭, and C♭
C♭ Major has B♭, E♭, A♭, D♭, G♭, C♭, and F♭

REVIEW
MAJOR KEY SIGNATURES

1. The Order of Sharps is: ____, ____, ____, ____, ____, ____, ____.

2. The Order of Flats is: ____, ____, ____, ____, ____, ____, ____.

3. If a key signature has three sharps, they will be ____, ____, and ____.

4. If a key signature has two flats, B♭ and E♭, the name of the key is ____ Major.

5. If a key signature has sharps, how far do you go up from the last sharp to find the name of the Major key? (Circle the answer.)

        A whole step   A third   A half step

6. Name these Major keys.

7. Write the key signatures for these keys.

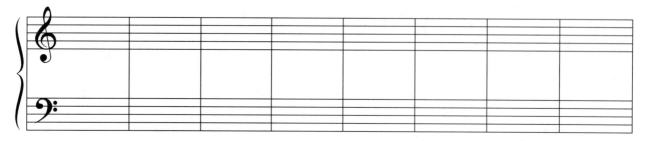

F♯ Major D Major C♭ Major E♭ Major C Major D♭ Major F Major E Major

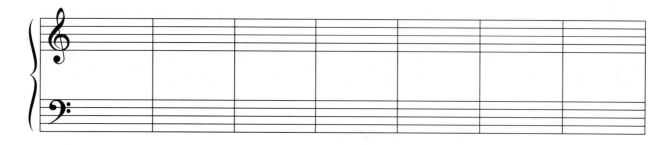

B Major   B♭ Major   G Major   C♯ Major   A♭ Major   G♭ Major   A Major

8. Match these key signatures with their names by drawing lines to connect them.

C Major B♭ Major A Major E♭ Major F♯ Major G Major D Major B Major

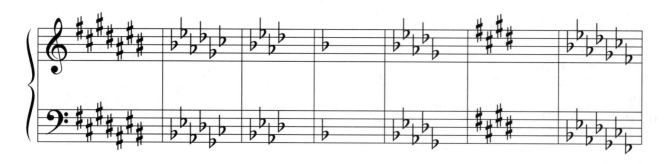

A♭ Major   D♭ Major   G♭ Major   C♭ Major   C♯ Major   F Major   E Major

LESSON 2
MAJOR SCALES

MAJOR SCALES have eight notes, which are each a step apart. They begin and end with notes of the same letter name, and have all the sharps or flats in the key signature of the key with the same name.

Example: **D Major Scale** begins and ends with the note "D," and has **F♯ and C♯.**

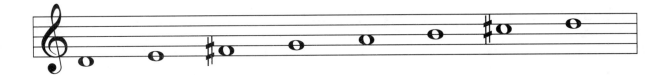

D MAJOR SCALE

1. Add the necessary sharps or flats to complete these scales. (Note: If the scale begins with a sharp or flat, it ends with a sharp or flat.) (The first one is done for you.)

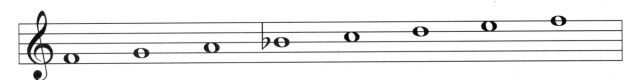

F Major Scale

G Major Scale

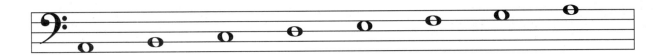

A Major Scale

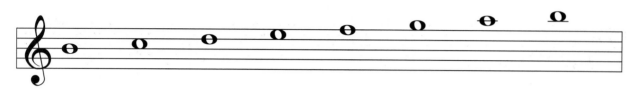

B Major Scale

D Major Scale

B♭ Major Scale

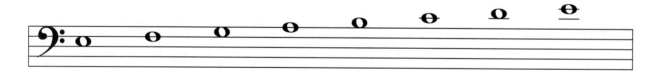

E Major Scale

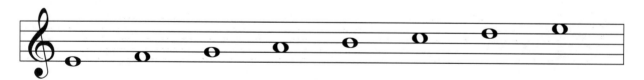

E♭ Major Scale

2. Write these scales.

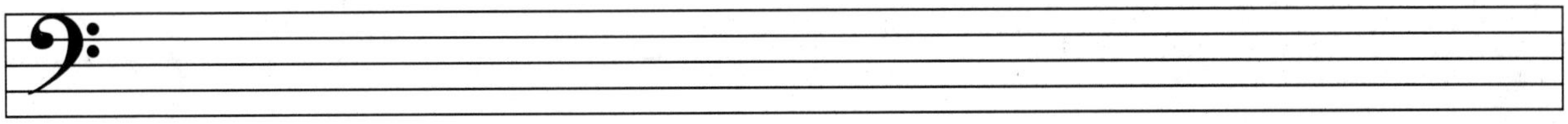

$9:$

C Major Scale

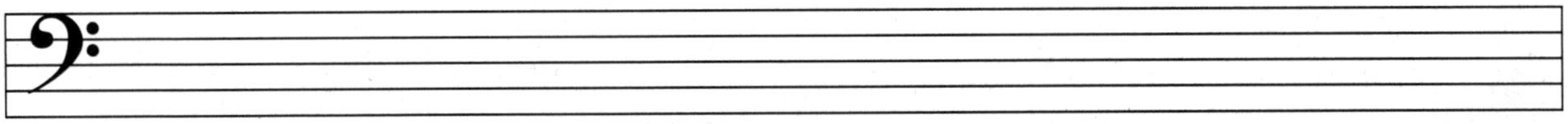

$9:$

B♭ Major Scale

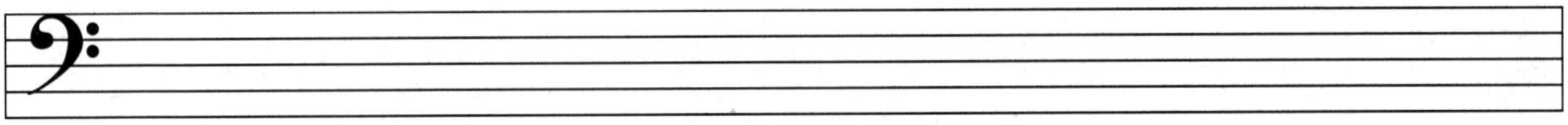

$9:$

D Major Scale

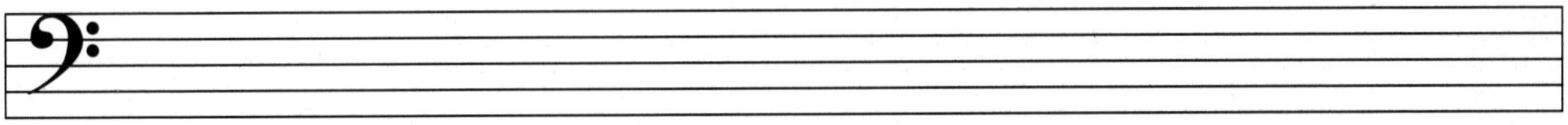

$9:$

E♭ Major Scale

$9:$

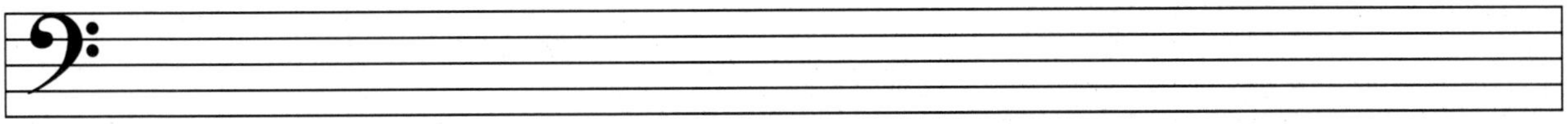

F Major Scale

G Major Scale

E Major Scale

A Major Scale

B Major Scale

LESSON 3
MINOR KEY SIGNATURES AND SCALES

Major key signatures have **RELATIVE MINORS.** The relative minor is found by going down three half steps from the Major key name.

KEY SIGNATURE FOR C MAJOR
THREE HALF STEPS BELOW C IS A
KEY OF A MINOR

One way to determine whether a composition is in the Major or minor key is to look at the last note of the piece. It is usually the same as the name of the key. (For example, a piece which is in the key of a minor will probably end on A.) Also, look at the music to find the note around which the music appears to be centered.

1. Write the name of the relative minors for the following Major keys. (Determine the relative minor by going <u>down</u> three half steps from the name of the Major key.) The first one is done for you.

    a. G Major   <u>   e minor   </u>

    b. C Major   <u>   </u>

    c. F Major   <u>   </u>

2. Give the name of the relative Major for each of the following minor keys. (Determine the relative Major by going <u>up</u> three half steps.) The first one is done for you.

    a. d minor   <u>   F Major   </u>

    b. e minor   <u>   </u>

    c. a minor   <u>   </u>

3. Name these <u>minor</u> keys. (Determine the Major key name, then go <u>down</u> three half steps to find the relative minor.) The first one is done for you.

     <u>   a minor   </u>   <u>   </u>   <u>   </u>

4. Write the key signatures for these minor keys. (Go <u>up</u> three half steps to find the relative Major, then write the key signature for that Major key.) The first one is done for you.

     e minor   d minor   a minor

5. Match these minor key signatures with their names.

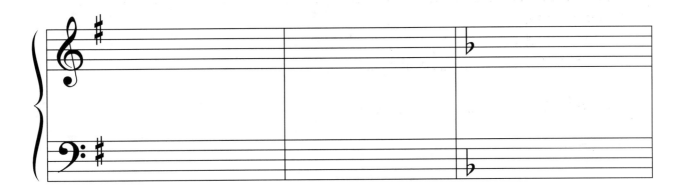

a minor   e minor   d minor

6. Memorize these minor key signatures.

    a. a minor has no sharps or flats (relative of C Major).
    b. e minor has F♯ (relative of G Major).
    c. d minor has B♭ (relative of F Major).

7. Tell the Major or minor key name for each of these examples.

a. From *Allegro non Tanto* by Turk. Key of _____ _____

III-22

b. From Etude by Gurlitt. Key of _____ _____

c. From *Arabesque* by Burgmuller. Key of _____ _____

c. From *A Little Song* by Kabalevsky. Key of _____ _____

d. From *Innocence* by Burgmuller. Key of _____ _____

Like Major scales, **MINOR SCALES** have eight notes, which are each a step apart. They begin and end with notes of the same letter name, and have all the sharps or flats in the key signature of the key with the same name.

There are several forms of minor scales. Two of these are **NATURAL MINOR** and **HARMONIC MINOR.**

NATURAL MINOR SCALES have only the sharps or flats which are in the key signature. For example, d natural minor scale begins and ends with the note "D," and has B♭.

D NATURAL MINOR SCALE

In **HARMONIC MINOR SCALES,** the seventh (7th) note is raised a half step, without changing the letter name of the note.

A HARMONIC MINOR SCALE

8. Add the necessary sharps or flats to complete these scales. (The first one is done for you.)

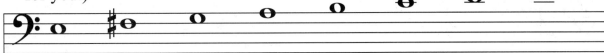

e natural minor scale

d harmonic minor scale

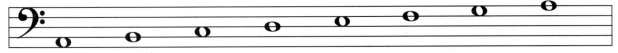

a harmonic minor scale

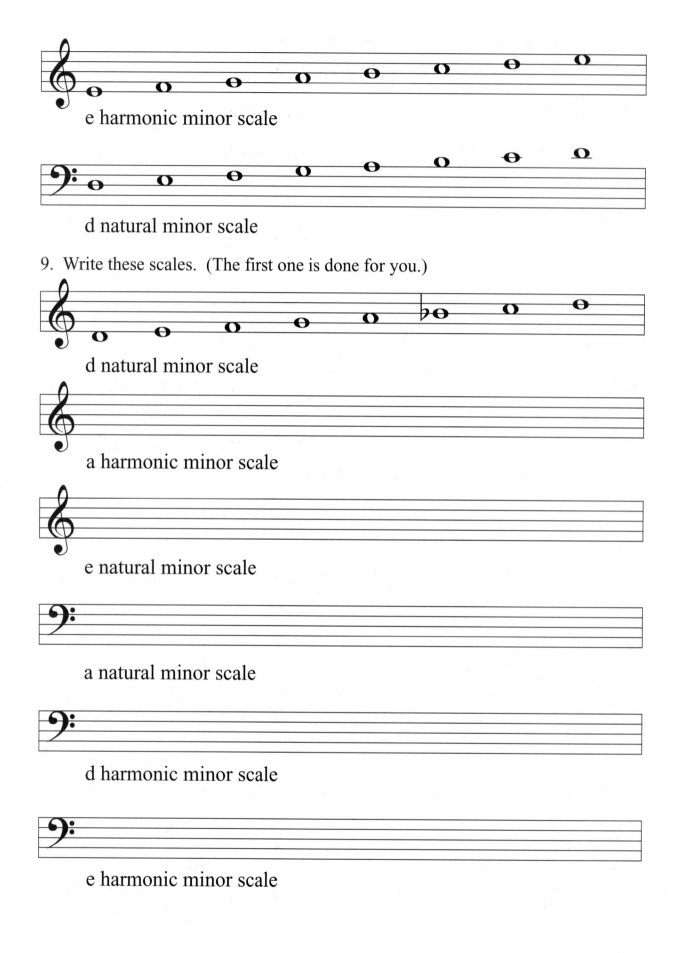

e harmonic minor scale

d natural minor scale

9. Write these scales. (The first one is done for you.)

d natural minor scale

a harmonic minor scale

e natural minor scale

a natural minor scale

d harmonic minor scale

e harmonic minor scale

LESSON 4
INTERVALS

An **INTERVAL** is the distance between two notes. Intervals are named with numbers.

When naming intervals, count the two notes that make the interval, and all the lines and spaces, or all the letter names, between them.

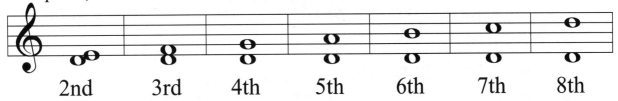

2nd   3rd   4th   5th   6th   7th   8th

If the top note of the interval is within the key of the bottom note, the interval is **Major** or **Perfect**. 2nds, 3rds, 6ths, and 7ths are Major, and 4ths, 5ths, and 8ths are Perfect.

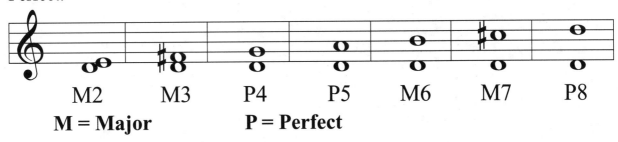

M2   M3   P4   P5   M6   M7   P8

M = Major   **P = Perfect**

1. Name these intervals. Give their qualities (Major or Perfect) and number names (2nd, 3rd, etc.). (The first one is done for you.)

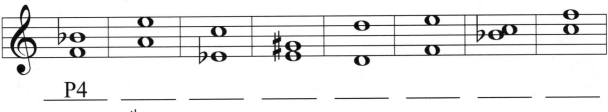

P4   ___   ___   ___   ___   ___   ___

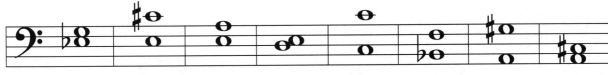

___   ___   ___   ___   ___   ___   ___

2. Write a note above the given note to complete these intervals. Be sure to put the sharps or flats from the key signature on the top note. (The first one is given.)

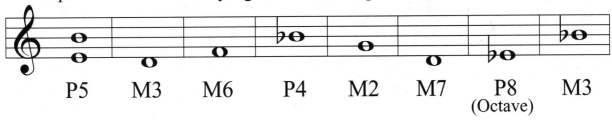

P5   M3   M6   P4   M2   M7   P8   M3
(Octave)

(2, continued)

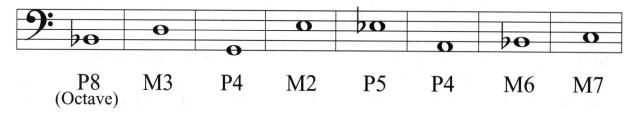

P8   M3   P4   M2   P5   P4   M6   M7

(Octave)

3. Name the circled intervals in the examples below. Be sure to check the key signature for sharps or flats! (The first one is done for you.)

a. From *Allegro non Tanto* by Turk.

b. From *Minuet* by Turk.

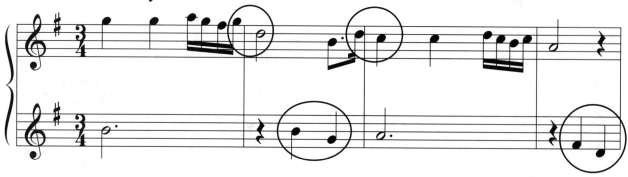

c. From *March in D* by J.S. Bach.

LESSON 5
MAJOR AND MINOR TRIADS

A **TRIAD** is a three note chord.

D MAJOR TRIAD

MAJOR TRIADS are made up of the first, third, and fifth notes of the Major scale with the same letter name. The bottom note of a Major triad in root position gives it its name.

D Major Scale   Block   Broken
D Major Triad

1. Name these Major triads. The first one is given.

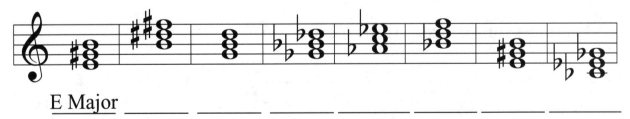

E Major _____ _____ _____ _____ _____ _____

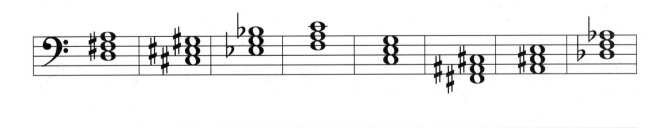

_____ _____ _____ _____ _____ _____

2. Write these triads. The first one is given.

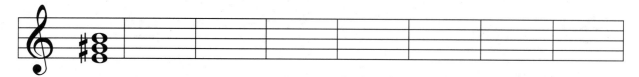

E Major A Major   B Major F Major   G Major E♭ Major F♯ Major G♭ Major

E Major B♭ Major E Major D Major C Major A♭ Major C♭ Major C♯ Major

To change a Major triad into a **MINOR** triad, lower the third or middle note a half step.

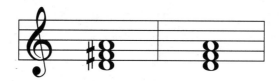

D Major Triad d minor Triad

3. Name these minor triads. The first one is given.

g minor _____ _____ _____ _____ _____ _____

_____ _____ _____ _____

4. Write these minor triads. The first one is given.

e♭ minor   b♭ minor   c♯ minor   b minor   g minor   a minor   a♭ minor   g♭ minor

f minor   c♭ minor   a minor   f♯ minor   d minor   e minor   c minor   e♭ minor

5. Name these triads with their letter names (A, B, C, etc.), and qualities (Major or minor). The first one is given.

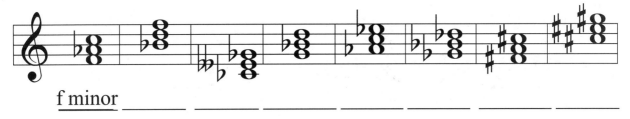

f minor ___ ___ ___ ___ ___ ___ ___

___ ___ ___ ___ ___ ___ ___

6. Write these triads. The first one is given.

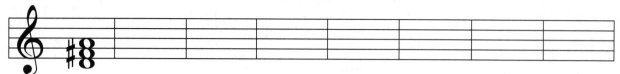

D Major Db Major ab minor F Major c# minor A Major d minor g minor

Cb Major Eb Major gb minor bb minor G Major e minor C Major F# Major

The following chart can help you remember the triads you have just studied.

C, F, and G Majors have all white keys; minors have a flatted third.

D, A, and E Majors have a sharp on the third; minors have all white keys.

Db, Eb, and Ab Majors have flats on the first and fifth, and a white key on the third; minors have three flats.

Gb and Cb Majors have three flats; minors have a flat on the first and fifth, and a double flat on the third.

F# and C# Majors have three sharps; minors have sharps on the first and fifth only.

Bb Major has a flat on the first; minor has flats on the first and third.

B Major has sharps on the third and fifth; minor has a sharp on the fifth only.

LESSON 6
TRIADS AND INVERSIONS

A **ROOT POSITION TRIAD** occurs when the note which names the triad is on the bottom. Root position triads are called 5/3 triads, because the intervals from the bottom note are a 5th and a 3rd. When labelling a triad in root position, only the letter name and quality are needed.

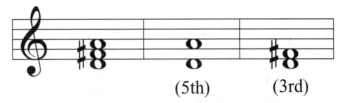

(5th)   (3rd)

D Major Root Position Triad
(D Major)

1. Name these root position triads with their letter names and qualities. (The first one is done for you.)

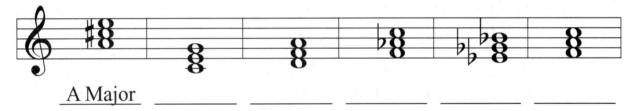

A Major _____ _____ _____ _____ _____

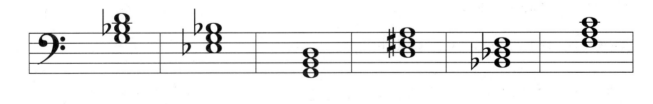

_____ _____ _____ _____ _____ _____

Count Triadica invites you to join him in his adventures using
PBJ's *Basics of Keyboard Theory Computer Activities, Levels 3-4.*
www.pbjmusic.com   teachme@pbjmusic.com

2. Write these root position triads.

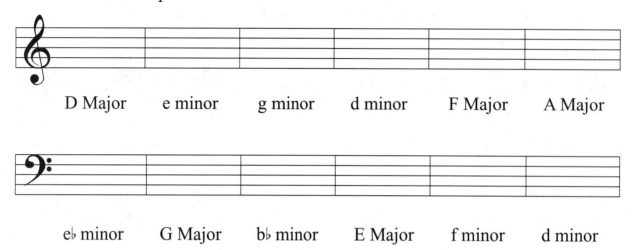

D Major   e minor   g minor   d minor   F Major   A Major

e♭ minor   G Major   b♭ minor   E Major   f minor   d minor

A **FIRST INVERSION TRIAD** occurs when the **third** or **middle** note of the triad is on the bottom. First inversion triads are called 6/3 triads, because when they are in their simplest position (with the notes close together) they contain the intervals of a 6th and a 3rd above the bottom note. In this simple position, the top note of the triad names it.

When labelling first inversion triads, the symbol "6" is used beside the name of the triad.

D Major
Root Position Triad

D Major
First Inversion Triad
(D Major ⁶)

(6th)   (3rd)

3. Circle the first inversion triads below.

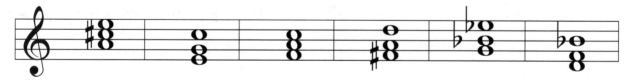

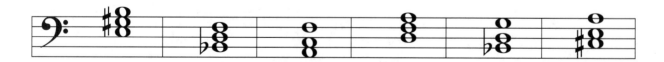

4. Name these first inversion triads with their letter names, qualities, and inversions. The first one is given.

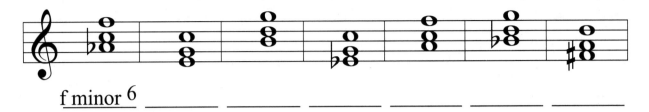

f minor 6 _____ _____ _____ _____ _____ _____

_____ _____ _____ _____ _____ _____

5. Write these first inversion triads. The first one is given.

c minor 6   F Major 6   G Major 6   C Major 6   g minor 6   f minor 6   d minor 6

F Major 6   c minor 6   g minor 6   G Major 6   C Major 6   f minor 6   D Major 6

A **<u>SECOND INVERSION TRIAD</u>** occurs when the **<u>fifth</u>** or **<u>top</u>** note of the triad is on the bottom. Second inversion triads are called 6/4 triads, because when they are in their simplest position (with the notes close together) they contain the intervals of a 6th and a 4th above the bottom note. In this simple position, the middle note of the triad names it.

When labelling second inversion triads, the symbol $\frac{"6"}{4}$ is used beside the name of the triad.

| D Major Root Position Triad (D Major) | D Major First Inversion Triad (D Major ^{6}) | D Major Second Inversion Triad (D Major $^6_4$) | (6th) | (4th) |

6. Circle the second inversion triads below.

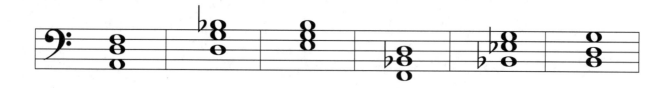

7. Name these second inversion triads with their letter names, qualities, and
   inversions. (The first one is done for you.)

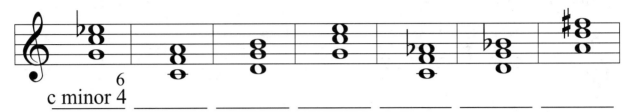

c minor $^6_4$ _____ _____ _____ _____ _____ _____

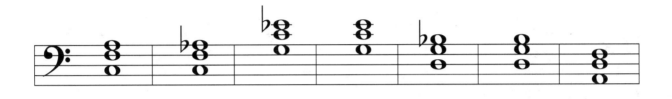

_____ _____ _____ _____ _____ _____

8. Write these second inversion triads. The first one is given.

g minor $^6_4$ C Major $^6_4$ F Major $^6_4$ c minor $^6_4$ f minor $^6_4$ G Major $^6_4$ d minor $^6_4$

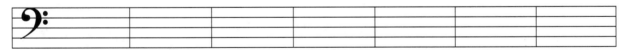

g minor $^6_4$ C Major $^6_4$ F Major $^6_4$ f minor $^6_4$ G Major $^6_4$ c minor $^6_4$ D Major $^6_4$

9. Write these triads in root position, first inversion, and second inversion. The first one is given.

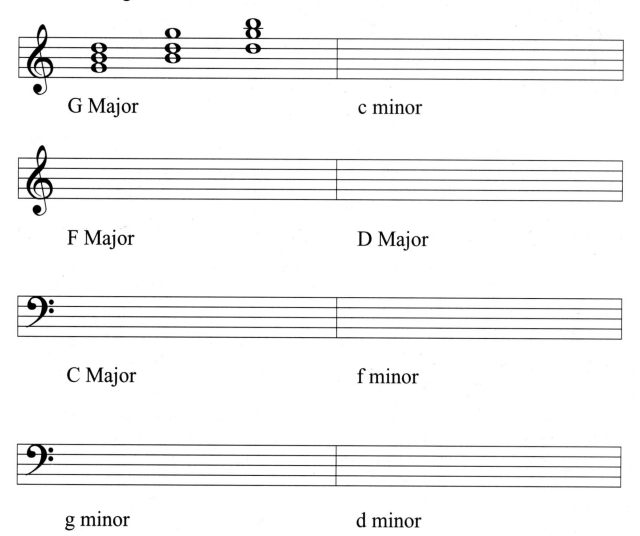

G Major   c minor

F Major   D Major

C Major   f minor

g minor   d minor

When naming triads within a piece of music, do the following:

1. Place all the sharps or flats from the key signature before the notes on the music.

2. Put the letters of the notes into root position (for example, F♯-D-A becomes D-F♯-A).

3. Determine the letter name and quality (Major or minor) of the triad.

4. Determine the inversion by looking at the lowest note of the chord in the bass clef part of the music.

Example: From *Hungarian Folk Song* by Bartok.

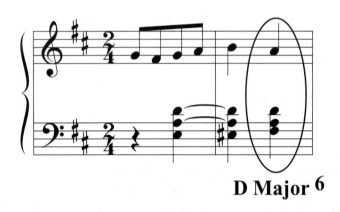

D Major 6

1. Place F♯ on the F.

2. The notes are F♯-A-D-A. Root position is D-F♯-A.

3. D Major triad.

4. F♯ is the lowest note; the triad is in first inversion.

5. D Major 6 triad.

10. Name the circled triads with their letter names, qualities, and inversions.

a. From *Hungarian Folk Song* by Bartok.

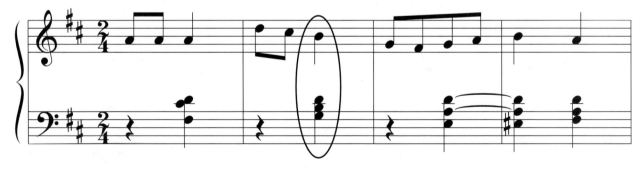

———

b. From *Etude in d minor* by Gurlitt.

c. From *Arabesque* by Burgmuller.

d. From *Sonatina, Op. 36, No. 1* by Clementi.

e. From *Sonatina, Op. 36, No. 1* by Clementi.

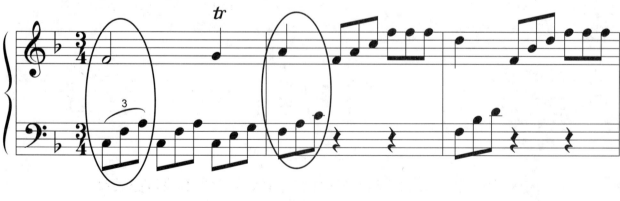

LESSON 7
PRIMARY TRIADS

A triad can be built on each note of the scale.

TRIADS BUILT ON THE NOTES OF D MAJOR SCALE

When building triads on scale tones, all of the sharps or flats that are in the scale must be added to the chords which have those notes.

Example: D Major Scale has F♯ and C♯. When writing the triads of D Major, every time an F or C appears in a chord, a sharp must be added to it. (See above example.)

Triads of the scale are numbered using Roman Numerals. Upper case Roman Numerals are used for Major triads, and lower case Roman Numerals are used for minor triads.

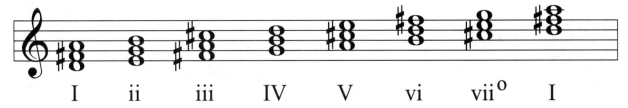

I   ii   iii   IV   V   vi   vii°   I

(The vii° chord is diminished. This means that the top and middle notes have been lowered a half step from Major.)

I, IV, and V are the **PRIMARY TRIADS**. In Major keys, these three triads are **Major**, and are the most commonly used chords for harmonizing tonal melodies. The chords are labelled with upper case Roman Numerals.

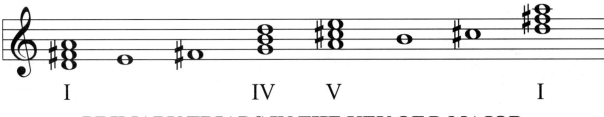

I   IV   V   I

PRIMARY TRIADS IN THE KEY OF D MAJOR

The **I** chord is called **TONIC.**

The **IV** chord is called **SUBDOMINANT**.

The **V** chord is called **DOMINANT**.

1. Circle the Primary Triads (Tonic, Subdominant, and Dominant) below, and label them with upper case Roman Numerals. (The first one is done for you.)

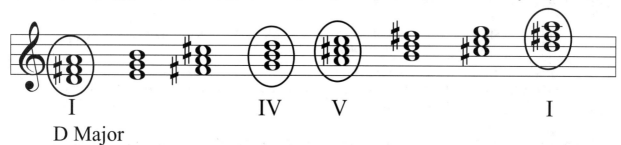

I   IV   V   I

D Major

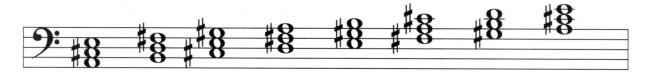

A Major

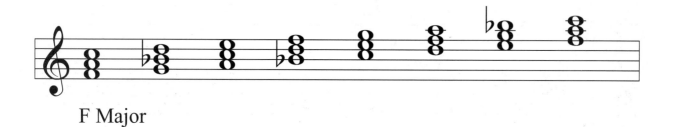

F Major

E Major

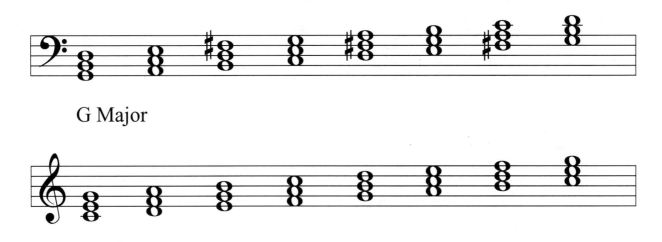

G Major

C major

2. Number the first, fourth, and fifth notes of these scales using Roman Numerals, then build the Primary Triads (Tonic, Subdominant, and Dominant) on those notes. Watch the clef signs! (The first one is done for you.)

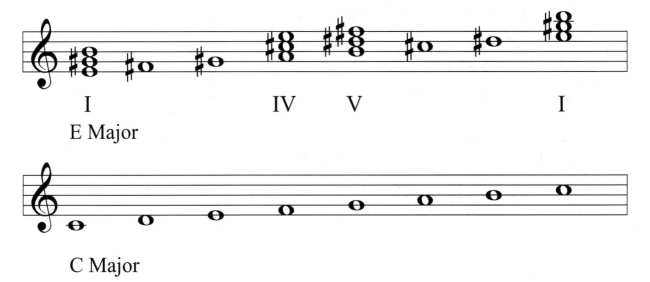

I   IV   V   I

E Major

C Major

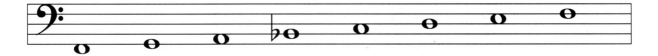

F Major

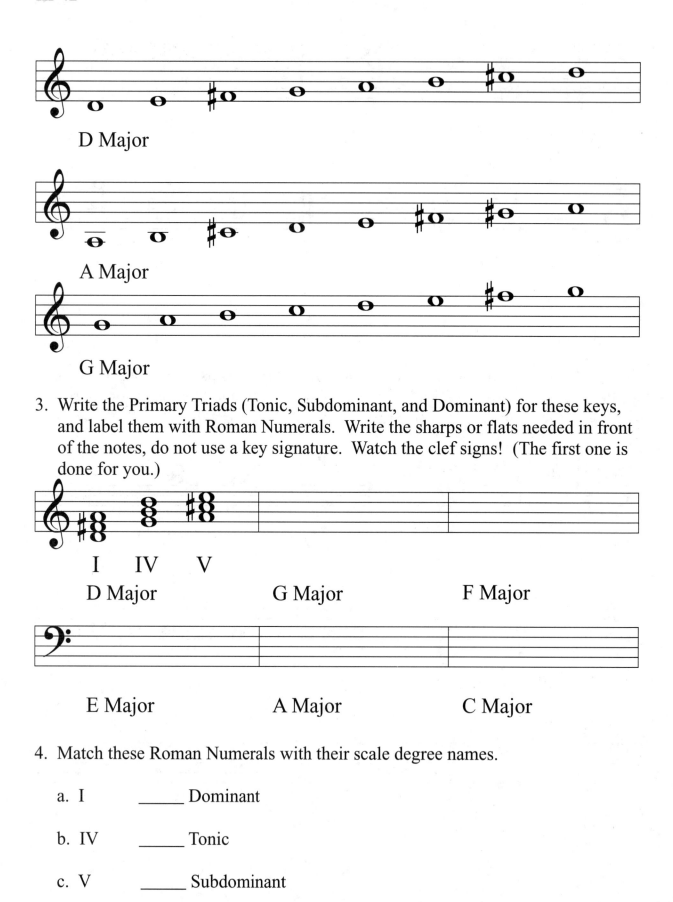

D Major

A Major

G Major

3. Write the Primary Triads (Tonic, Subdominant, and Dominant) for these keys, and label them with Roman Numerals. Write the sharps or flats needed in front of the notes, do not use a key signature. Watch the clef signs! (The first one is done for you.)

    I   IV   V

D Major   G Major   F Major

E Major   A Major   C Major

4. Match these Roman Numerals with their scale degree names.

    a. I   _____ Dominant

    b. IV   _____ Tonic

    c. V   _____ Subdominant

When naming the Primary Triads within a composition, do the following:

1. Place all the sharps or flats from the key signature before the notes on the music.

2. Put the letters of the notes into root position (for example, F#-D-A becomes D-F#-A).

3. Determine the letter name and quality (Major or minor) of the triad.

4. Name the key of the piece. Count up from the name of the key to find the Roman Numeral name for the chord.

Example: From *Hungarian Folk Song* by Bartok.

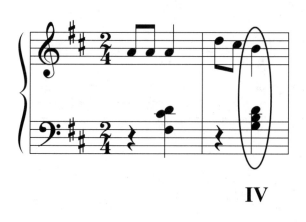

IV

1. This chord does not have any sharps or flats.

2. The notes are G-B-D-B.

3. G Major Triad

4. The piece is in the key of D Major. G is four (4) notes above D. Label the chord with the Roman Numeral IV.

5. Name the circled triads in the examples below with their Roman Numerals.

a. From *Play Time* by Bartok. Key of _____ _____

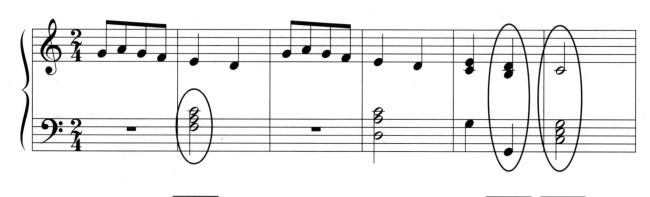

_____   _____ _____

b. From *March* by J.S. Bach. Key of _____ _____

_____

c. From *March* by J.S. Bach. Key of _____ _____

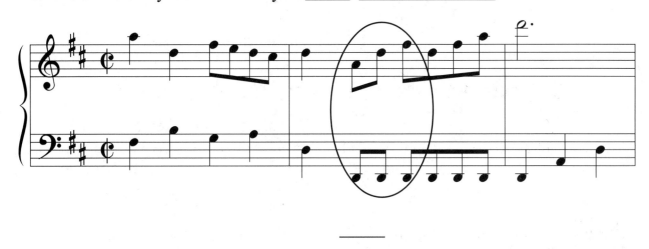

_____

d. From *Sonatina, Op. 36, No. 1*, by Clementi. Key of _____ _____

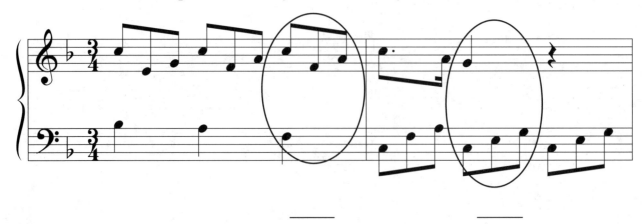

_____   _____

LESSON 8
AUTHENTIC, HALF, AND PLAGAL CADENCES

A **CADENCE** is a closing or ending for a musical phrase, made up of a combination of chords. There are many types of cadences. Three common cadences are:

AUTHENTIC, HALF, AND PLAGAL CADENCES

An **AUTHENTIC CADENCE** consists of a V chord followed by a I chord:

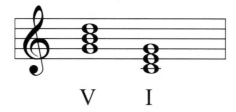

V   I

AUTHENTIC CADENCE IN C MAJOR

1. Write Authentic Cadences in these Major keys, and label the chords with Roman Numerals. (The first one is done for you.)

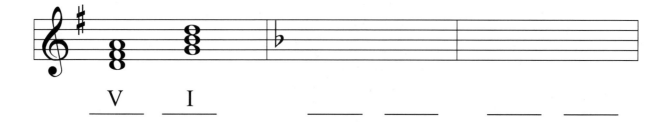

V   I

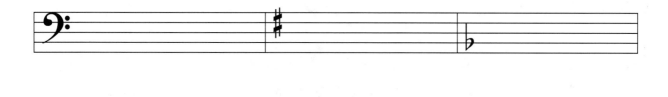

A **PLAGAL CADENCE** consists of a IV chord followed by a I chord:

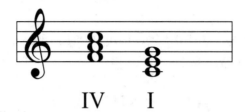

IV   I

PLAGAL CADENCE IN C MAJOR

2. Write Plagal Cadences in these Major keys, and label the chords with Roman Numerals. (The first one is done for you.)

IV   I

A **HALF CADENCE** ends on a V chord:

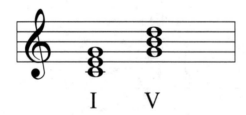

I   V

HALF CADENCE IN C MAJOR

3. Write Half Cadences using I-V in these Major keys, and label the chords with Roman Numerals. (The first one is done for you.)

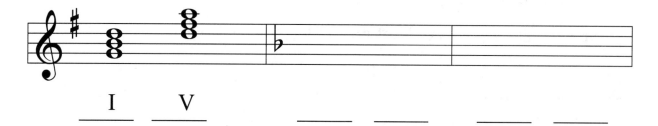

       I   V   ___ ___   ___ ___

___ ___   ___ ___   ___ ___

4. Label the chords of each of these cadences with Roman Numerals, then put the name of the type of cadence (Authentic, Half, or Plagal) on the line below the Roman Numerals. (The first one is done for you.)

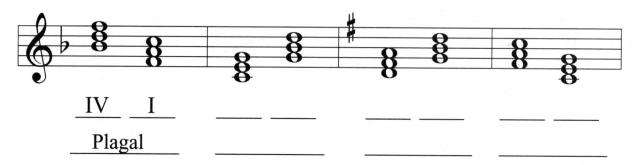

  IV   I   ___ ___   ___ ___   ___ ___

  Plagal   ___   ___   ___

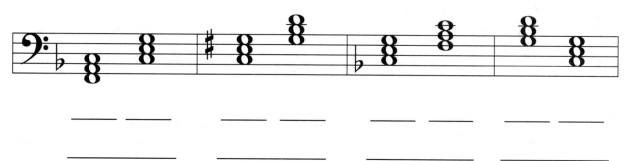

___ ___   ___ ___   ___ ___

___   ___   ___

III-48

5. Label the last two triads of these examples (the circled ones) with their Roman Numerals, and tell the type of cadence. (The first one is done for you.)

a. From *Sonatina, Op. 36, No. 1*, by Clementi. Key of ___F___ ___Major___

Type of Cadence: ___Authentic___

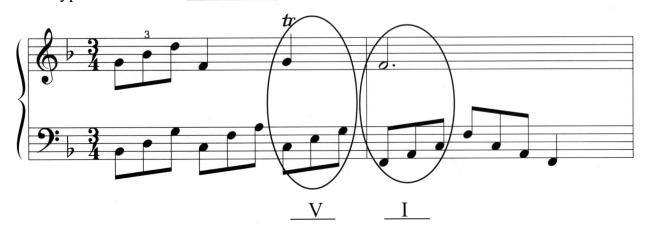

___V___   ___I___

b. From *Playtime* by Bartok. Key of _____ _____

Type of Cadence: _____

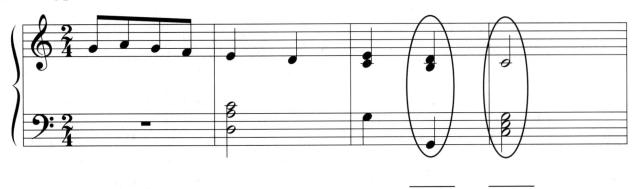

_____   _____

c. From *Sonatina* by Beethoven. Key of _____ _____

Type of Cadence: _____

_____   _____

REVIEW
WORDS USED IN LESSONS 1-8

Study these words before doing *Review: Lessons 1-8.*

1. **Interval:** The distance between two notes, named with numbers.

2. **Key Signature:** The sharps or flats at the beginning of a piece of music. (There are Major and minor key signatures.)

3. **Scale:** Eight (8) notes in order (for example, C-D-E-F-G-A-B-C). Scales need the sharps or flats from the key signature with the same letter name.

4. **Triad:** A chord with three different notes in it.

5. **Root Position:** A triad written in a position so that the note which names it is on the bottom of the triad.

6. **Inversion:** A triad written in a position other than root position, so that the note which names it is not on the bottom.

7. **First Inversion:** A triad written with the third (or middle) note on the bottom.

8. **Second Inversion:** A triad written with the fifth (or top) note on the bottom.

9. **Primary Triads:** The I, IV, and V chords.

10. **Scale Degree Names:** Tonic (I), Supertonic (ii), Mediant (iii), Subdominant (IV), Dominant (V), Submediant (vi), Leading Tone (vii⁰).

11. **Cadence:** A closing or ending for a phrase of music, made up of two or more chords.

12. **Authentic Cadence:** A cadence made up of the V chord followed by the I chord (V-I).

13. **Plagal Cadence:** A cadence made up of the IV chord followed by the I chord (IV-I).

14. **Half Cadence:** A cadence which ends on the V chord.

This page has purposely been left blank.

REVIEW
LESSONS 1-8

1. Name these Major keys.

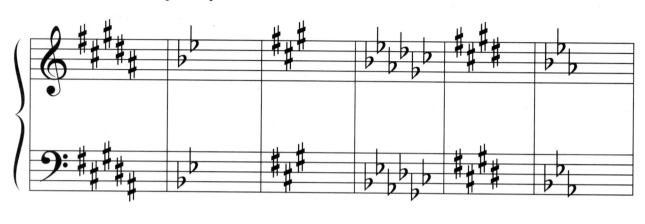

_____ _____ _____ _____ _____ _____

2. Write the key signatures for these keys in both clefs.

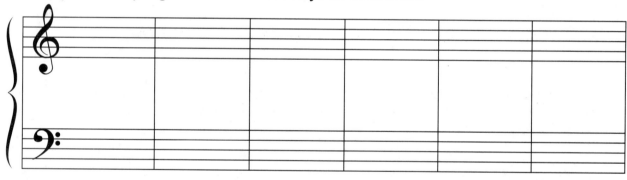

Eb Major   d minor   Gb Major   F# Major   D Major   G Major

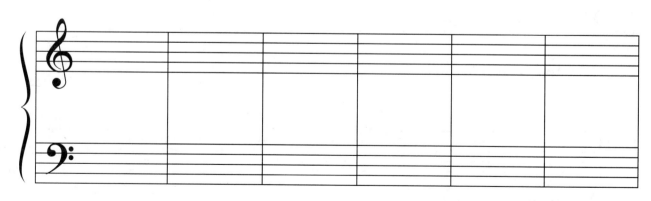

Bb Major   a minor   F Major   Cb Major   e minor   C# Major

3. Write these scales. (The first one is done for you.)

D Major

A Major

E Major

B♭ Major

e natural minor

a harmonic minor

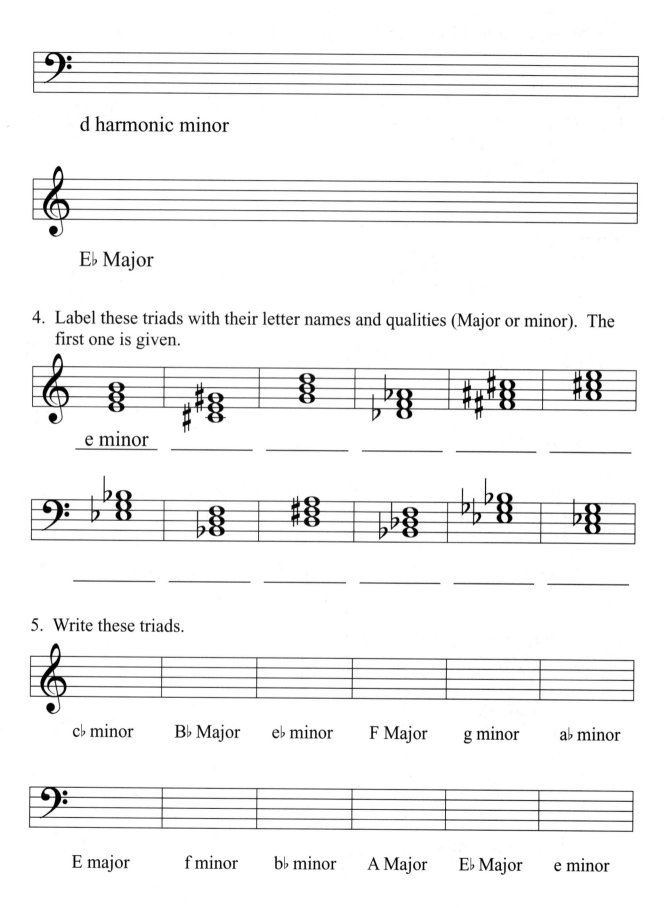

d harmonic minor

Eb Major

4. Label these triads with their letter names and qualities (Major or minor). The first one is given.

e minor

5. Write these triads.

cb minor   Bb Major   eb minor   F Major   g minor   ab minor

E major   f minor   bb minor   A Major   Eb Major   e minor

6. Label these triads with their letter names, qualities (Major or minor), and inversions. The first one is given.

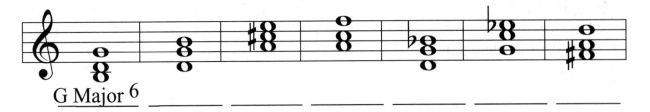

G Major 6 ___ ___ ___ ___ ___ ___

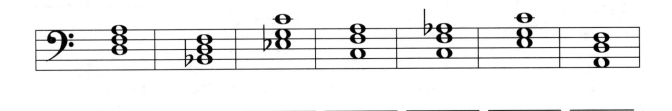

___ ___ ___ ___ ___ ___

7. Write these triads.

C Major 6   g minor 6/4   F Major   G Major 6   f minor 6   c minor   d minor 6

F Major 6   c minor 6/4   G Major   g minor 6   f minor 6/4   c minor 6   D Major 6/4

8. Name these intervals. (The first one is done for you.)

P4 ___ ___ ___ ___ ___ ___

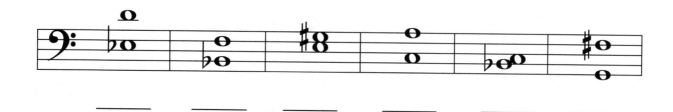

___ ___ ___ ___ ___ ___

9. Write a note above the written note to complete these intervals. (The first one is done for you.)

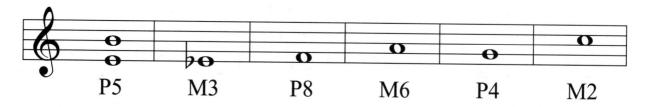

P5   M3   P8   M6   P4   M2

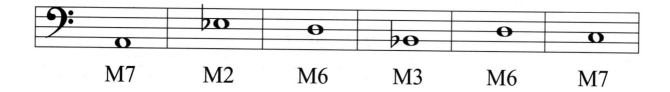

M7   M2   M6   M3   M6   M7

10. Write the primary triads for the following Major keys, and label the triads with Roman Numerals. (The first one is done for you.)

I   IV   V

11. Label these chords using Roman Numerals, then tell what type of cadence each is. (The first one is done for you.)

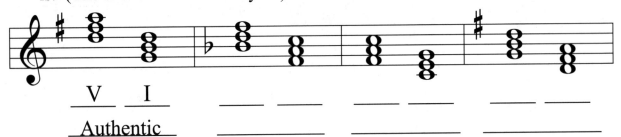

V   I   ____ ____   ____ ____   ____ ____

Authentic   _____   _____   _____

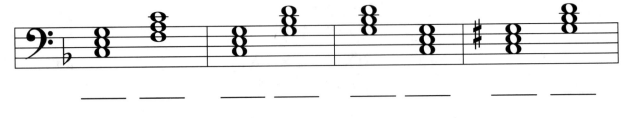

____ ____   ____ ____   ____ ____   ____ ____

_____   _____   _____   _____

12. Match these scale degree names with their Roman Numerals.

_____ Dominant   a. IV

_____ Subdominant   b. I

_____ Tonic   c. V

LESSON 9
TIME SIGNATURES

The **TIME SIGNATURE** for a piece of music is found at the beginning, next to the key signature. The time signature is made up of two numbers:

Sometimes, the letter **C** or **₵** is used instead of numbers.

C stands for 4/4, or **Common Time**.

₵ stands for 2/2, or **Alla Breve**.

The **top number** of the time signature tells **how many beats or counts are in each measure.**

The **bottom number** tells **which type of note receives one beat or count.**

  2 = 2 beats or counts per measure
  4 = Quarter note (♩) receives one beat or count

  6 = 6 beats or counts per measure
  8 = Eighth note (♪) receives one beat or count

When the bottom number of a time signature is a "4," a quarter note (♩) receives one beat or count. The following chart shows how many beats to give these notes or rests:

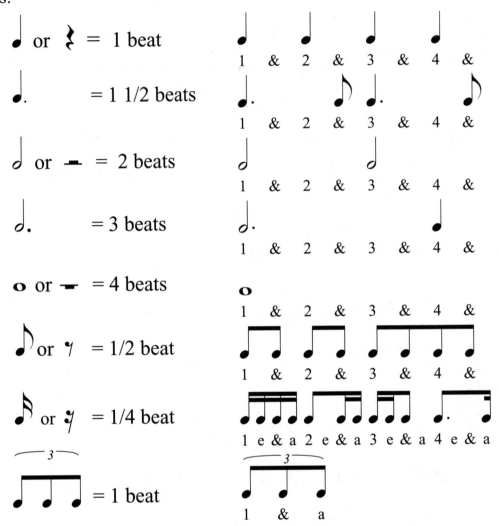

An **UPBEAT** occurs when an incomplete measure begins the piece. The last beat or beats are "borrowed" from the final measure of the piece and placed at the beginning. The counts used for the upbeat measure will be the last numbers of the time signature. The first full measure begins with count number 1.

Example:

When a piece of music is in $\frac{2}{4}$ the first beat of each measure is emphasized.

When a piece of music is in $\frac{3}{4}$ the first beat of each measure is emphasized.

When a piece of music is in $\frac{4}{4}$ the first beat of each measure is emphasized, and the third beat of each measure is emphasized slightly.

1. Fill in the blanks. (The first one is done for you.)

2 = <u>2 beats (counts) per measure. The first beat is emphasized.</u>
4 = <u>Quarter note receives one beat or count.</u>

3 = _____
4 = _____

4 = _____
4 = _____

C stands for _____

¢ stands for _____

5 = _____
4 = _____

7 = _____
4 = _____

2. Write the counts for these phrases, and place accents on the beats which should be emphasized. The first measure is done for you. Notice how the counts for the treble clef notes line up with the counts for the bass clef notes.

a. From *Song of the Hussars* by Kohler.

4   1 & 2 & 3   4 &

b. From *Musette* by J.S. Bach.

c. From *Minuet* by C.P.E. Bach.

d. From *Sonatina, Op. 36, No. 1* by Clementi.

e. From *Sonatina* by Andre.

f. From *Burleske* by L. Mozart.

When the bottom number of a time signature is a "2," a half note (♩) receives one beat or count. The following chart shows how many beats to give these notes or rests:

♩ or ▬ = 1 beat

♩. = 1 1/2 beats

o or ▬ = 2 beats

♪ or ૪ = 1/2 beat

♪ or ૪ = 1/4 beat

When a piece of music is in $\frac{2}{2}$, the first beat of each measure is emphasized.

When the time signature for a piece of music has an 8 on the bottom, an eighth note receives one beat.

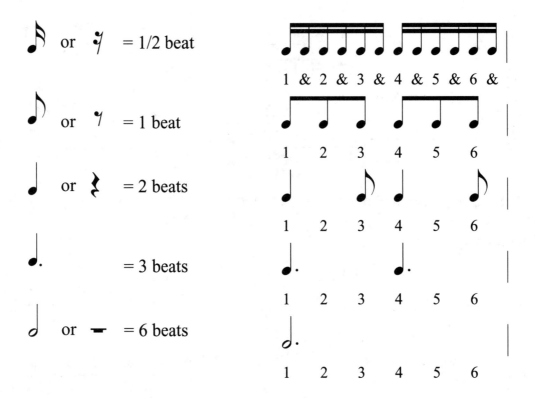

6/8 is the most common time signature which uses an eighth note as one beat.

When a piece of music is in 6/8, the first beat of each measure is emphasized, and the fourth beat receives a slight emphasis.

3. Fill in the blanks.

6
8 = _____ beats in a measure.
= eighth note (♪) receives _____ beat.

9
8 = 9 beats in a _____.
= _____ receives one beat.

12
8 = _____ beats in a measure.
= _____ receives one beat.

2
2 = 2 beats in a _____.
= _____ receives one beat.

3
2 = _____ beats in a measure.
= Half note receives _____.

12
2 = _____ in a measure.
= _____ receives one beat.

4. Write the counts for these phrases. (The first measure is done for you.)

a. From *Musette* by J.S. Bach.

b. From *Sonatina in G* by Beethoven.

c. From *Aylesford Piece* by G.F. Handel.

d. From *Rondo* by Mozart.

e. From *Old German Dance* (Composer Unknown).

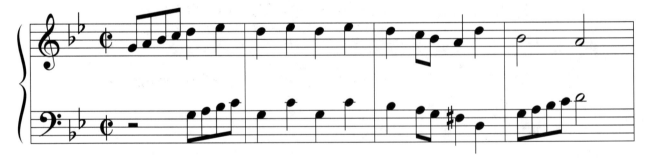

LESSON 10
SIGNS AND TERMS

Music often contains many signs and terms other than just notes and rhythms. Memorize the ones listed below.

A Tempo: Return to the original tempo (the speed with which you began the piece).

Accent: Play the note louder than the others.

Accelerando: Accelerate; gradually faster.

Adagio: Slowly.

Allegro: Fast or quick.

Andante: A moderate walking tempo.

Crescendo: Gradually louder.

D.C. al Fine: Go back to the beginning of the piece, and play until you see the word *Fine*.

or 𝄐 ❋ **Damper Pedal:** Push the pedal located on the right of the three (or two) piano pedals.

Decrescendo or Diminuendo: Gradually softer.

Dolce: Sweetly.

Dynamics: Letters or symbols which tell how loud or soft the music should sound.

f **Forte**: Loud.

ff **Fortissimo**: Very loud.

fff **Fortississimo:** Very, very loud.

Fermata: Hold the note longer than its value.

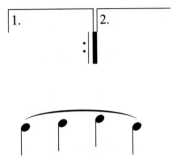

First and Second Ending: Play the piece with the first ending (under the 1. , repeat the piece, and the second time you play it, skip the first ending and play the second ending (under the 2.).

Legato Sign: Play smoothly, connect the notes.

Lento: Slowly.

mf **Mezzo Forte:** Medium loud.

mp **Mezzo Piano:** Medium soft.

Moderato: A moderate or medium tempo.

Molto: Much, very.

Octave Sign: Play the notes an octave higher (or lower if under the notes) than where they are written.

p **Piano:** Soft.

pp **Pianissimo:** Very soft.

ppp **Pianississimo:** Very, very soft.

Phrase: A musical sentence, often four measures long.

Poco: Little.

||: :|| Repeat Sign: Repeat that section of music. Go back to the nearest repeat signs, or to the beginning of the piece if there are none.

Ritardando *(ritard., rit.)*: Slow down gradually.

sfz or *sf* **Sforzando:** A sudden, sharp accent.

Slur: Connect the first note to the second, then release the second note.

Spiritoso: Spirited; with spirit.

Staccato: Play crisply or detached.

Stress or Tenuto: Play the note slightly louder than the others; stress the note.

Tempo: the speed at which to play a piece.

 **Tie:** Hold the second note, do not repeat it.

Tre Corde: Release the Una Corda Pedal (the pedal on the left).

Una Corda: Often abbreviated U.C. in music. Press the left or soft pedal.

Vivace: Quick, lively.

1. Match these terms and symbols with their definitions.

_____ *p*

_____ *ff*

_____ *mp*

_____ 8va ♩

_____ *f*

_____ *mf*

_____ Dynamics

_____ *pp*

_____ *ppp*

_____ *fff*

_____ *sfz*

a. Mezzo Piano: Medium soft.

b. Pianissimo: Very soft.

c. Piano: Soft.

d. Fortissimo: Very loud.

e. Mezzo Forte: Medium loud.

f. Symbols which tell how loud or soft the music should sound.

g. Forte: Loud.

h. Play the notes an octave higher than written.

i. Fortississimo: Very, very loud.

j. Sforzando: A sudden, sharp accent.

k. Pianississimo: Very, very soft.

---

2. Match these terms and symbols with their definitions.

_____

_____

_____

_____

_____

_____

a. Legato: Connect the notes.

b. Repeat Sign: Repeat the music.

c. Slur: Connect fhe first note to the second note, then release the second note.

d. Fermata: Hold the note longer than its value.

e. First and Second Ending.

f. Staccato: Detached.

3. Match these terms and symbols with their definitions.

_____

_____

_____ Phrase

_____ Ped. *

_____ D.C. al Fine

_____ Ritardando (*rit.*)

_____ A Tempo

a. Use the damper pedal (the pedal on the right).

b. A musical sentence, often four measures long.

c. Stress or tenuto: stresss the note, or play it louder than the others.

d. Accent: Play the note louder than the others.

e. Slow down gradually.

f. Return to the original tempo (the speed with which you began the music).

g. Go back to the beginning and play until you see the word *fine.*

4. Match these terms and symbols with their definitions.

_____ Allegro   a. A moderate walking tempo.

_____ Andante   b. Gradually louder.

_____ Vivace   c. Gradually softer.

_____ Adagio   d. A moderate or medium tempo.

_____ Moderato   e. Quick or lively.

_____ <   f. Fast, quick.

_____ >   g. Slowly.

5. Match these terms and symbols with their definitions.

_____ Una Corda   a. Gradually faster.

_____ Accelerando   b. Use soft pedal (left pedal).

_____ Spiritoso   c. Sweetly.

_____ Molto   d. Little.

_____ Dolce   e. Much; greatly.

_____ Poco   f. Release the soft pedal (left pedal).

_____ Tre Corde   g. With spirit.

LESSON 11
MOTIF; REPETITION AND SEQUENCE

A **MOTIF** (or **MOTIVE**) is a short group of notes used in a piece of music. The composer uses this motif as the main idea of the music and repeats it in many different ways.

Beethoven's *Symphony No. 5* uses this motif:

It is repeated, with variations, several times at the beginning of the Symphony:

This motif is used often throughout the Symphony. It would be helpful to listen to the entire first movement of Beethoven's Symphony No. 5, and you will hear this motif used in many interesting ways.

REPETITION takes place when the motif is repeated immediately, exactly the way it was the first time it occured.

Das Ballet by Turk uses repetition. The repetition is circled.

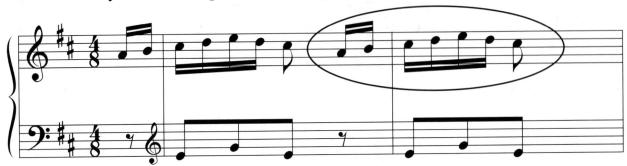

SEQUENCE occurs when the motif is repeated immediately, on a different note, usually a 2nd or 3rd higher or lower.

Minuet in F, K.5, by Mozart, uses sequence. The sequence in the example below is circled.

1. Circle the Repetition or Sequence in each example below, then write the type of technique (Repetition or Sequence) on the line above the music. (The first one is done for you.)

a. From *Contradance* by Mozart. _____Sequence_____

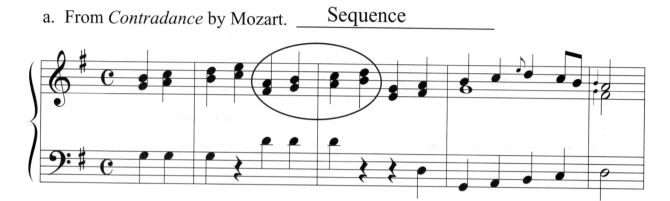

b. From *Minuet in F*, K. 4, by Mozart. _____

c. From *Springtime* by Bartok. _____

d. From *Fanfare Minuet* by Duncombe. _____

REVIEW
LESSONS 9-11

1. Fill in the blanks.

$\frac{2}{4}$ = _____ beats per measure, emphasize beat _____.
= _____ receives one beat.

$\frac{6}{8}$ = _____ beats per measure, emphasize beats _____ and _____.
= _____ receives one beat.

$\frac{3}{4}$ = 3 beats per _____, emphasize beat _____.
= Quarter note receives _____.

$\frac{4}{4}$ = _____ beats per measure, emphasize beats _____ and _____.
= _____ receives one beat.

𝄴 stands for _____ or _____.

𝄵 stands for _____ or _____.

2. Write the counts for these measures, and place accents on the notes which should be emphasized. (The first measure is done for you.)

a. From *Minuet* by Telemann.

b. From *The Wild Horseman* by Schumann.

3. Define these words and symbols.

1.   _____

2.   _____

3.   _____

4.   _____

5.   _____

6.   _____

7.   _____

8. *sfz*   _____

9. _____

10. _____

11. Dynamics _____

12. D.C. al Fine _____

13. A Tempo _____

14. Ritardando (*rit.*) _____

15. *f* _____

16. *mp* _____

17. *pp* _____

18. *ff* _____

19. *mf* _____

20. *p* _____

21. _____

22. _____

23. *fff* _____

24. *ppp* _____

25. Tempo _____

26. Vivace _____

27. Andante _____

28. Moderato _____

29. Allegro _____

30. *sf* _____

31. 𝄟 ❀ _____

32. Alla Breve _____

33. Common Time _____

34. Accelerando _____

35. Adagio _____

36. Spiritoso _____

37. Phrase _____

38. Molto _____

39. Una Corda _____

40. Poco _____

41. Tre Corde _____

4. Tell which compositional technique (Repetition or Sequence) is used in each
   example below, write the answer on the line beside the title, and circle the
   section that is the repetition or sequence.

a. From *Minuet in F, K. 4,* by Mozart. _____

b. From *Fanfare Minuet* by Duncombe. _____

Score: _____ **REVIEW TEST** Perfect Score = 56
Passing Score = 39

1. Write the following key signatures. (8 points)

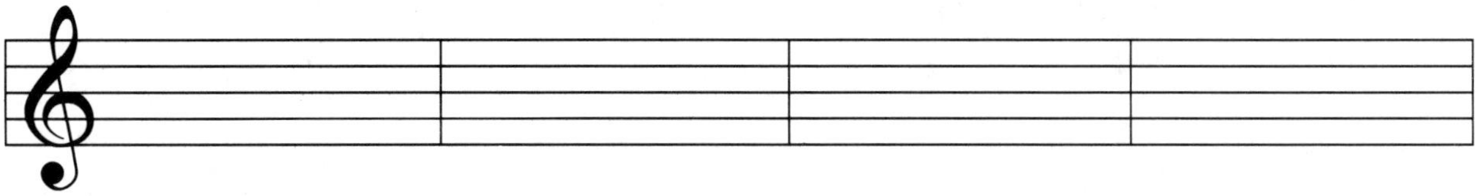

Bb Major   A Major   E Major   e minor

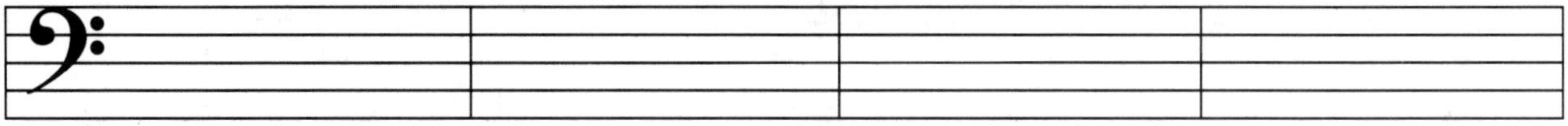

d minor   Eb Major   F Major   C Major

2. Write the following scales. (3 points)

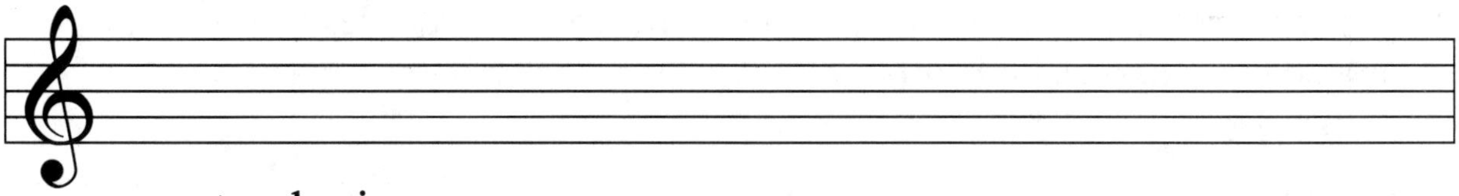

a natural minor

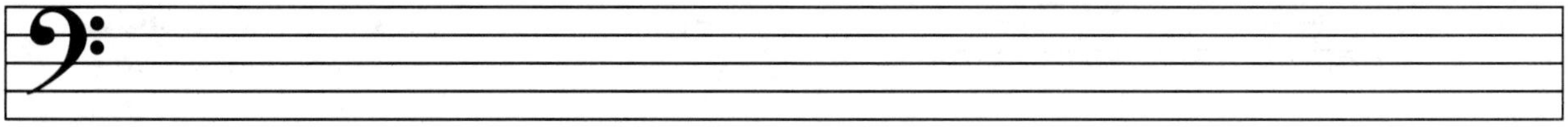

E Major

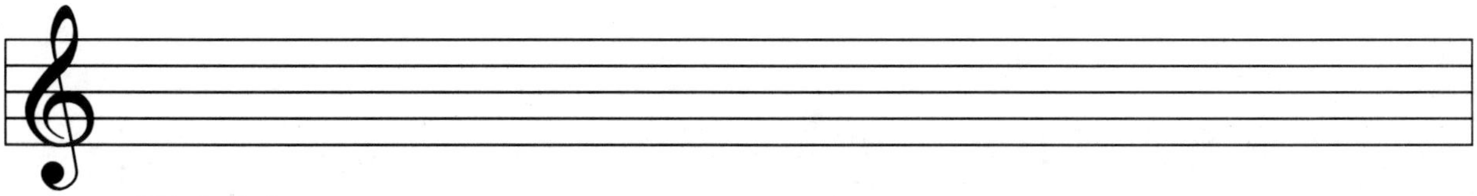

Bb Major

3. Write the Primary Triads for the key of F Major. The I chord (Tonic) is given.
   (2 points)

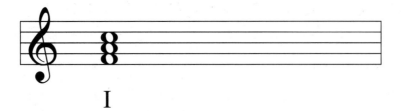

I

4. Give the Roman Numeral and letter names of the Primary Triads from the
   example in question 3. The I chord (Tonic) is given. (4 points)

ROMAN NUMERAL   **LETTER NAME**

_____ I _____   _____ F Major _____

_____   _____

_____   _____

5. Write the Roman Numerals under the chords for the cadences below. Then,
   match the cadences in the first row with their names in the second row.
   (9 points)

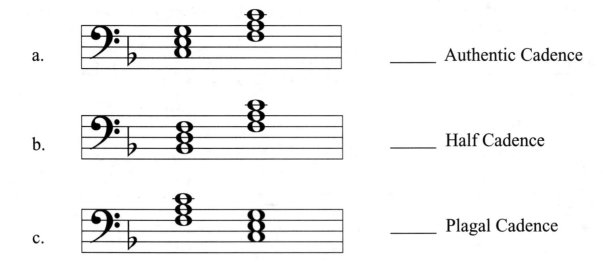

a.   _____ Authentic Cadence

b.   _____ Half Cadence

c.   _____ Plagal Cadence

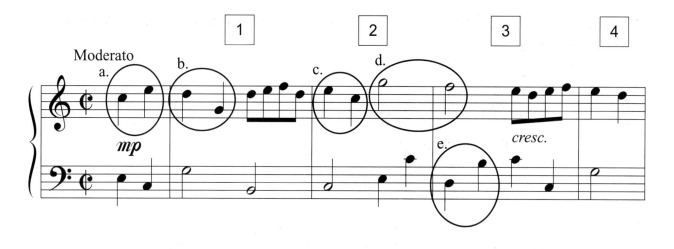

6. The example above is from *Gavotte* by Telemann. Answer these questions about the music. (12 points)

a. What does the term "Moderato" mean? _____

b. What does the dynamic marking *mp* mean? (Give the English meaning.)

   _____

c. What is the key or tonality of the piece? _____

d. What does ₵ stand for? (Circle the answer.)

   Common Time   Alla Breve   3/4 Time

e. Which beat(s) will be emphasized? _____

f. The rhythm for the first two measures of the treble clef are given below. Write the counts under the notes.

g. What dynamic term is used in measure 3? _____

   What is its English meaning? _____

h. Name the intervals circled on the music. (The first one is done for you.)

   a. __M3__   b. _____   c. _____   d. _____   e. _____

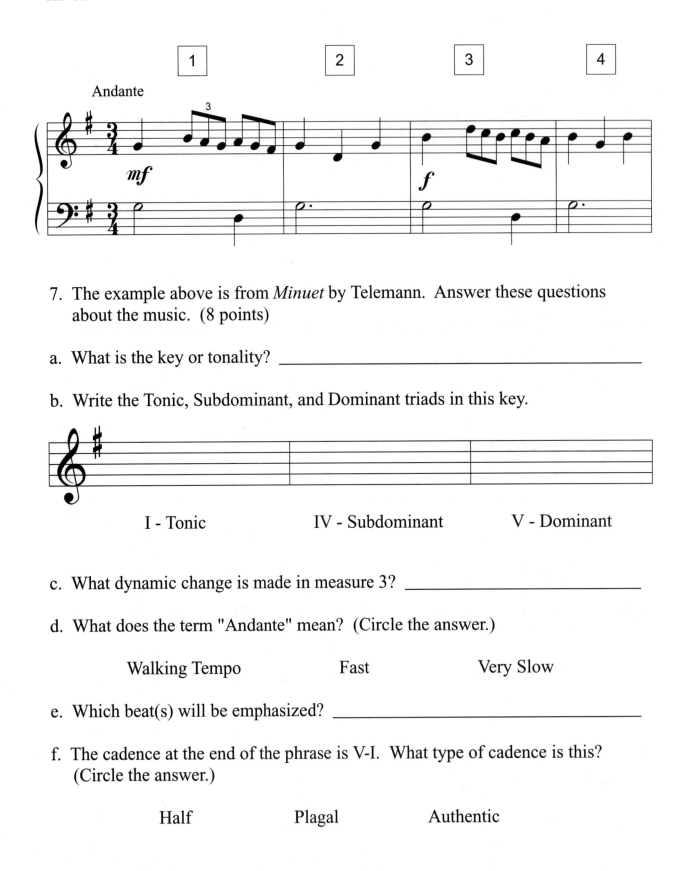

7. The example above is from *Minuet* by Telemann. Answer these questions about the music. (8 points)

a. What is the key or tonality? _____

b. Write the Tonic, Subdominant, and Dominant triads in this key.

            I - Tonic   IV - Subdominant   V - Dominant

c. What dynamic change is made in measure 3? _____

d. What does the term "Andante" mean? (Circle the answer.)

            Walking Tempo   Fast   Very Slow

e. Which beat(s) will be emphasized? _____

f. The cadence at the end of the phrase is V-I. What type of cadence is this? (Circle the answer.)

            Half   Plagal   Authentic

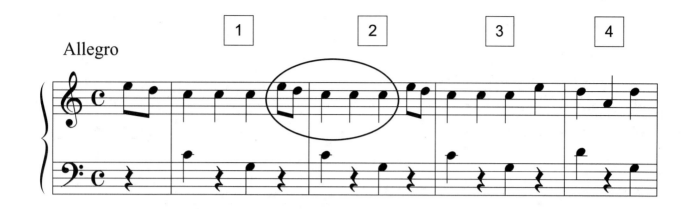

8. The example above is from *March* by Shostakovich. Answer these questions about the music. (4 points)

a. What does the term "Allegro" mean? _____

b. Look at the circled notes in the treble clef part of the music. What compositional technique is used here? (Circle the answer.)

               Repetition   Sequence

c. What does **C** stand for? _____

d. What is the key or tonality? _____

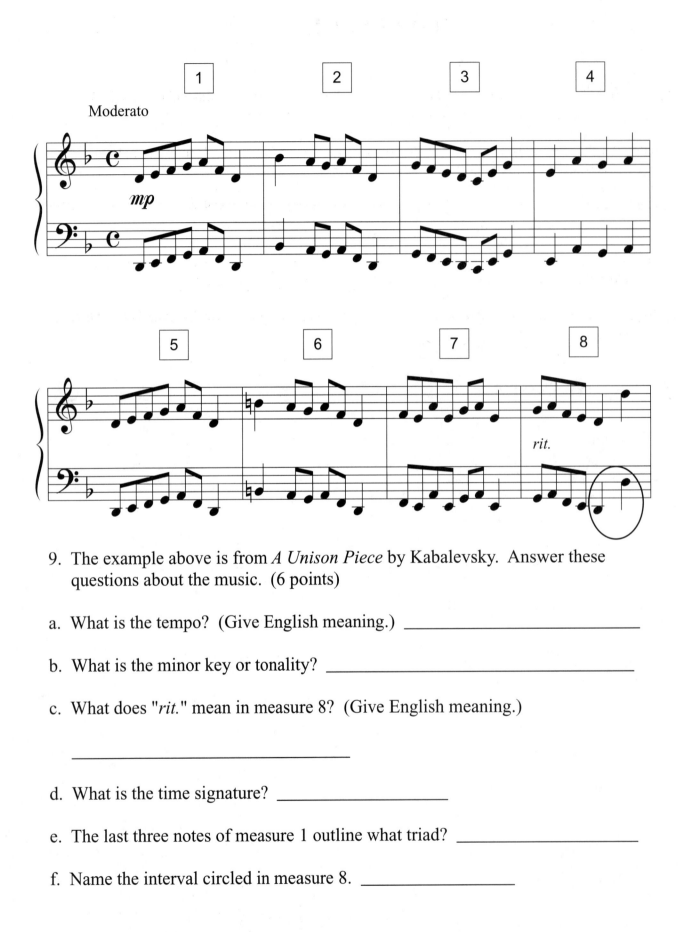

9. The example above is from *A Unison Piece* by Kabalevsky. Answer these questions about the music. (6 points)

a. What is the tempo? (Give English meaning.) _____

b. What is the minor key or tonality? _____

c. What does "*rit.*" mean in measure 8? (Give English meaning.)

_____

d. What is the time signature? _____

e. The last three notes of measure 1 outline what triad? _____

f. Name the interval circled in measure 8. _____

REFERENCES

Apel, Willi. *Harvard Dictionary of Music, Second Edition.* Cambridge, Massachusetts: Belknap Press of Harvard University Press, 1972.

Arnold, Denis, ed. *The New Oxford Companion to Music, Volumes 1 and 2.* New York: Oxford University Press, 1983.

Music Teachers' Association of California. *Certificate of Merit Piano Syllabus, 1992 Edition.* San Francisco: Music Teachers' Association of California, 1992.

Music Teachers' Association of California. *Certificate of Merit Piano Syllabus, 1997 Edition.* Ontario, Canada: The Frederick Harris Music Company, Limited, 1997.

Sadie, Stanley, ed. *The New Grove Dictionary of Music and Musicians.* Washington, D.C.: Grove's Dictionaries of Music Inc., 1980.

BASICS OF KEYBOARD THEORY

Workbooks by Julie McIntosh Johnson
Computer Activities by Nancy Plourde

ORDER FORM

NAME_____

ADDRESS_____

CITY_____STATE_____ZIP_____

COUNTY_____PHONE_____

QTY	ITEM	COST	TOTAL
	PREPARATORY LEVEL	8.95	
	LEVEL I	8.95	
	LEVEL II	8.95	
	LEVEL III	8.95	
	LEVEL IV	8.95	
	LEVEL V	8.95	
	LEVEL VI	9.95	
	LEVEL VII	10.45	
	LEVEL VIII	11.45	
	LEVEL IX	11.95	
	Level X (Advanced)	11.95	
	ANSWER BOOK	10.95	
	COMPUTER ACTIVITIES LEVELS PREP-2, Mac/PC	49.95	
	COMPUTER ACTIVITIES LEVELS 3-4, Mac/PC	39.95	
	COMPUTER ACTIVITIES LEVELS 5-6, PC Only	49.95	

UPS Shipping Rates:
    1-5 Books.........$4.00
    6-10 Books.......$5.00
    11 or more........$6.00

Sub-Total	
Calif. Residents: Sales Tax	
Shipping	
TOTAL	

Make checks payable to:
J. JOHNSON MUSIC PUB.
5062 Siesta Ln.
Yorba Linda, CA 92886
(714) 961-0257

THANK YOU FOR YOUR ORDER

BASICS OF KEYBOARD THEORY

Workbooks by Julie McIntosh Johnson
Computer Activities by Nancy Plourde

ORDER FORM

NAME_____

ADDRESS_____

CITY_____STATE_____ZIP_____

COUNTY_____PHONE_____

QTY	ITEM	COST	TOTAL
	PREPARATORY LEVEL	8.95	
	LEVEL I	8.95	
	LEVEL II	8.95	
	LEVEL III	8.95	
	LEVEL IV	8.95	
	LEVEL V	8.95	
	LEVEL VI	9.95	
	LEVEL VII	10.45	
	LEVEL VIII	11.45	
	LEVEL IX	11.95	
	Level X (Advanced)	11.95	
	ANSWER BOOK	10.95	
	COMPUTER ACTIVITIES LEVELS PREP-2, Mac/PC	49.95	
	COMPUTER ACTIVITIES LEVELS 3-4, Mac/PC	39.95	
	COMPUTER ACTIVITIES LEVELS 5-6, PC Only	49.95	

UPS Shipping Rates:
1-5 Books.........$4.00
6-10 Books.......$5.00
11 or more........$6.00

Sub-Total	
Calif. Residents: Sales Tax	
Shipping	
TOTAL	

Make checks payable to:

J. JOHNSON MUSIC PUB.
5062 Siesta Ln.
Yorba Linda, CA 92886
(714) 961-0257

THANK YOU FOR YOUR ORDER